INTERNATIONAL
GARDEN
PHOTOGRAPHER
OF THE YEAR

IMAGES OF A GREEN PLANET

CONTENTS

Design: Luke Bowman, Spingold Design & Print Ltd.
Design liaison: Linda McGlinchey.
Proofreading: James McGlinchey and Gregory Brooks.
Editor: Curtis McGlinchey.

A catalogue record for this book is available from the
British Library.

ISBN: 978-0-9934529-2-5

The contents of this book are believed correct at the
time of printing. Nevertheless, Garden World Images
Ltd cannot be held responsible for any errors or
omissions or for changes in the details given in this
book or for the consequences of any reliance on the
information provided by the same. This does not affect
your statutory rights.

Printed and bound in Wales, Great Britain
by Gomer Press.

www.igpoty.com

SPONSORS & SUPPORTERS

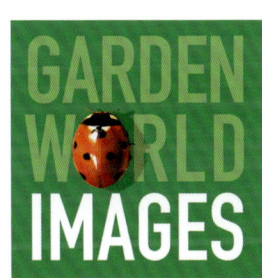  

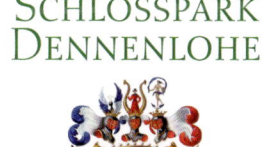

Die Gärten von Schloss Trauttmansdorff
I Giardini di Castel Trauttmansdorff
The Gardens of Trauttmansdorff Castle

 de hortus

Hortus Botanicus Amsterdam - anno 1638

INTRODUCTION

By Tony Kirkham, Head of the Arboretum,
Gardens and Horticultural Services, Royal Botanic Gardens, Kew

As judge of the Trees, Woods & Forests category in International Garden Photographer of the Year over the past ten years, I am still amazed and overwhelmed by the quality and standard of the many images placed before me. It is an extremely difficult task to judge them, as every image that I see has a different story to tell and is a potential winner. The bold imagination of the person behind the camera who compiles the image through the lens is outstanding, and the content and composition of these photographs must be the envy of many other photographers and tree experts like myself.

In my everyday work, whether it is at home in the Royal Botanic Gardens, Kew or if I am visiting gardens and arboreta around the world or looking at trees in natural woodlands and forests, I am constantly looking for the perfect shot – a tree in pristine surroundings with the perfect background and the perfect light and colour that I can use to illustrate my next article in a technical journal or reference book. This international competition gives me the inspiration to keep trying and to keep hunting for that perfect image, that perfect specimen.

I am sure that it is often about being in the right place at the right time, and I wonder if, when photographers find the ideal model in a tree, they then spend months or years revisiting the scene in different seasons with varying weather and lighting conditions to capture the subject in its seasonal entirety, ensuring every aspect and every facet has been documented.

This truly is an international competition and recently whilst leading a garden tour around Monserrate Palace and Park in Sintra, Portugal, I was rewarded by viewing the outdoor gallery of the exhibition of Competition 10. I was so proud to be able to explain to my group that I was the judge of the Trees, Woods & Forests category. Members of the group then spent the next half an hour viewing the photographs on display before we ventured off, on our way to see the specimen trees in the garden.

On my kitchen wall at home I have a large photograph of a beech tree in a woodland; it is a previous winner from the Trees, Woods & Forests category. It shows every part of the tree, from the buttressed root plate and the trunk, to the very tips of the upper canopy. It is surrounded by its woodland friends and I never get tired of looking at it.

I hope that this book of images from Competition 11 gives you the same joy and inspiration that it will give to me.

FOREWORD

By Roy Lancaster CBE VMH,
Plantsman, Gardener, Author, Broadcaster

Yes, I do admit to having photographed plants, people and places on visits to gardens and nurseries and on my travels to the world's wild places over the last 60 years, but I have never regarded myself nor ever pretended to be a serious practitioner, although I do still enjoy the advice and encouragement of those who are.

As a result of my endeavours I now share an office at home with a daunting battery of green cabinets housing thousands of potentially redundant colour slides, to which, in the last ten years, I have added a great number of digital images, all of which were taken for the purposes of illustrating my lectures and to a lesser degree, my articles and books.

A mere glance at the award-winning images selected in previous years convinces me that the contributors are of a special breed. They are blessed with an acute understanding of camera technology, a gunslinger's reaction to the unexpected and a gambler's intuition in choosing the right place at the right time, succeeding in capturing something most of us would die for; if only once in our lives. There is, however, one basic thing I share with these photographers, and it is that of the observer and recorder.

I have always believed that knowledge should be shared and that the pursuit of knowledge, like charity, begins at home, on one's doorstep. That's how my fascination with plants and the world's flora and fauna started – aged 14 in a cotton town in northern England. Even today, amongst my most treasured possessions are: a hand lens (x20), binoculars (8x42), a notebook and yes, a camera. With these I can observe and record most things I encounter, from little to large, the near and far, from the past to the present. They are my constant companions on my travels and are close to hand when I am in my garden quietly watching, listening, waiting.

Like many others I have taken great joy from viewing images from the competition, intrigued by the hint or suggestion of something familiar, something hidden, something else which caught the photographer's eye. Some of the images have left me gasping or guessing, some plants or places I have myself seen or visited, while others speak to me of unfulfilled wishes, loss, triumphs, hope. Most of all these images speak to me of a belief in the future. I am a born optimist and as such I urge IGPOTY to continue its journey of discovery, highlighting and celebrating all that is precious and beautiful on this green planet of ours. Ignorance we can change but apathy is the real challenge and neither must be allowed to prevail.

The judging of the International Garden Photographer of the Year took place over a period of two months from November to December 2017. Each photograph entered was scrutinised and assigned a ranking by individual judges during this blind judging process. These were then tallied and carried forward to a series of group judging sessions held at studios in Soho, London. High-resolution image files were requested from shortlisted entrants and a final set of judging decisions took place.

We thank all the judges for their dedication and thoroughness in assessing a very wide range of entries from all over the world.

JUDGES

• Tyrone McGlinchey, Managing Director of International Garden Photographer of the Year and Garden World Images Ltd

• Philip Smith, Founder of the International Garden Photographer of the Year

• Katie Weaver, Visitor Programmes Co-ordinator, Royal Botanic Gardens, Kew

• Tony Kirkham, Head of Arboretum and Horticultural Services, Royal Botanic Gardens, Kew

• Chris Lacey, National Trust Photographic Manager

• Clare Foggett, Editor, *The English Garden* magazine

• Benedict Brain, Editor, *Digital Camera* magazine

• Jürgen Becker, garden photographer

• Tracy Calder, Features Editor, *Amateur Photographer* magazine

• Carol Sharp, photographer

• John Humphrey FRPS, photographer

• Judith Klute, Art Director, Floramedia

• Sam Stewart, News Picture Editor, *The Times* newspaper

• Sabine Freifrau von Süsskind, Schlosspark Dennenlohe

EXHIBITION

The International Garden Photographer of the Year exhibition is formed from the competition winners. The exhibition tours a range of venues in the UK, Europe and worldwide, including: the Royal Botanic Gardens, Kew, various National Trust venues, Hortus Botanicus in Amsterdam, the Gibraltar Botanic Gardens and Schloss Dyck in Germany to name but a few.

THANKS

Tyrone McGlinchey, Managing Director of International Garden Photographer of the Year would like to thank:

• The Royal Botanic Gardens, Kew

• The National Trust

• The Royal Photographic Society

• Floramedia

• All exhibition partners

• Spingold Design & Print

• *The English Garden* magazine

• Photographers and supporters

• The IGPOTY team

• Michael Warren

• Richard Garner

WORKSHOPS

International Garden Photographer of the Year runs workshops at exhibition venues throughout the UK.

The sessions are open to anyone who wants to improve their garden and plant photography at whatever level of experience. For further details visit www.igpoty.com

CATEGORIES

Photographers can enter single images (within four slots) or portfolios of six images in any of the following categories with the associated briefing in mind.

WILDFLOWER LANDSCAPES

Flowers that were once widespread across fields, meadows and woods are now rare and some have become extinct in the wild. Bring this to the world's attention through your photography of plants in the landscape.

TREES, WOODS & FORESTS

We celebrate the tree in all its diverse forms. From the gnarled old oak to the mighty redwood, we are inviting you to show us how important trees are in our lives and in the health of our planet.

BREATHING SPACES

This category celebrates open spaces and the places where we love to relax and enjoy the feeling of well-being. It could be that people are the subject of your photography or it could be animals or plants; perhaps a landscape, a wide vista or a favourite hideaway.

THE BEAUTY OF PLANTS

Achieving great images of plants and flowers requires skill, passion and commitment. This category celebrates the ephemeral beauty of the plant – from seed to flower. Plant portraiture is all about capturing the very essence, or character of a plant. The judges will be looking for spot on technique and original artistic views of your subject.

BEAUTIFUL GARDENS

Visiting a garden is a great day out for many of us. We can stand and admire the work of gardeners who have dedicated themselves to creating a personal paradise for the enjoyment of themselves and others. You can enter images from gardens in any part of the world, from Tokyo to Tuscany, Montréal to Melbourne.

THE BOUNTIFUL EARTH

Mother Earth provides the food and medicine we need to survive. We celebrate the gifts of the earth, from the allotment to the wild medicinal herb, from the crops on which we depend to the home-grown tomato plant pot on the windowsill. Judges will look for images that connect people to the earth and show the essential part that plants play in our world.

GREENING THE CITY

On our crowded planet, town gardens, parks, open spaces and city nature reserves create conditions for a surprising variety of plants and wildlife to thrive. The judges will also look for images that celebrate the adaptability and importance of plants in an urban environment.

WILDLIFE IN THE GARDEN

In a world where natural habitats are being depleted, gardens are a haven for wildlife. The wild creatures that use our gardens and parks can become familiar companions, or welcome rare visitors.

ABSTRACT VIEWS

Whether infrared, innovative use of light, a special lens or filter. Abstract Views is about tapping into a different side of plants and gardens. It's time to enter a parallel world of artistic expression with limitless possibilities.

OUTDOOR LIVING

From natural swimming pools and decking, to landscaping and gazebos, judges will be paying close attention to how the photographer has presented the relationship between the organic and the man-made.

YOUNG GARDEN PHOTOGRAPHER OF THE YEAR

Entrants aged 17 and younger were invited to enter single images into any of the above categories. The title of Young Garden Photographer of the Year was awarded to the best single image.

AWARDS

The International Garden Photographer of the Year title was awarded to the photographer for the best single image overall. The overall winner is voted on from one of the main category First Places. These are not combined awards.

A First, Second and Third award was given for each category. In addition, a number of photographs in each category were judged to be Finalist. A number of photographs were also selected as Highly Commended and Commended in each category. A selection of these and the winning photographs from the International Garden Photographer of the Year competition will be exhibited at the Royal Botanic Gardens, Kew and other venues.

PORTFOLIOS

The best overall category themed Portfolio was awarded First Place and a gold medal from the Royal Photographic Society. Runner up prizes were awarded to the portfolios judged Second and Third. Portfolios are run in conjunction with the Royal Photographic Society.

PHOTO PROJECTS

Photo Projects are stand-alone competitions with separate prizes that give photographers the chance to explore selected skills and techniques. There are three annual Photo Projects: Black & White, Macro Art and Still Life.

SPECIAL AWARDS

A number of special awards are run every competition year in collaboration with our partners and supporters. These awards help bring the plants, gardens and green spaces of a specific theme, person or place onto the world stage.

SOCIAL MEDIA

Find us on:

 @igpoty

 @igpoty

@igpoty

INTERNATIONAL GARDEN PHOTOGRAPHER OF THE YEAR

MARCIO CABRAL

Marcio has captured a spectacular vision of plant life in the cerrado, displaying the beautiful flowers of Paepalanthus chiquitensis, stretching out on countless filaments towards the first light of the rising sun. It is artistically and technically brilliant, deploying superb use and understanding of equipment, post-capture processes, colour and exposure. It has the ability to make us feel novelty and wonder, as if experiencing plant life on this planet for the very first time. As ecosystems such as the Brazilian cerrado are under threat, this image urges us all to document, understand and protect our vulnerable landscapes, with even greater passion.

Tyrone McGlinchey FLS FRSA
Managing Director of International
Garden Photographer of the Year

MARCIO CABRAL

1st Place, Overall Winner

Cerrado Sunrise

Alto Paraíso de Goiás, Goiás, Brazil

📷 Canon EOS 5DS R, Nikkor 14-24mm lens, 2sec at f/16, ISO 100. Tripod, Fotodiox lens adapter, reverse neutral density graduated filter. Post-capture: basic image management.

The *Paepalanthus chiquitensis* is a special plant, endemic to South America with main occurrence in the cerrado region of Brazil. The plant itself is not considered endangered, however the accelerated advance of monoculture plantations (for example soya) in this region is causing concern. It is critical to shine a light on the wonder of these plants and take steps to preserve the unique beauty of the cerrado ecosystem. I intensified the natural glow of sunrise by increasing the contrast between the flowers and grass.

YI FAN
<small>2ND PLACE</small>

Spirit of the Holy Mountain
Baima Snow Mountain, Yunnan Province, China

📷 Canon EOS 5D Mark III, Canon 16-35mm lens, 1/80sec at
f/14, ISO 125. Post-capture: focus stacked 11 images,
basic image management.

With peak elevation of over 5000m, the heavenly
Baima Snow Mountain is regarded as a sacred
place by Tibetan Buddhists. The beauty and rarity
of this *Saussurea laniceps* add to a natural sense
of reverence for this special place. It is the most
effective (and collected) snow lotus species used in
both Tibetan and Chinese folk medicine.

SIMON HATHAWAY

3RD PLACE

Siam Tulips
Pa Hin Ngam National Park,
Chaiyaphum Province, Thailand

Nikon D700, Nikkor 17-35mm lens, 1/1250sec at f/8, ISO 200.
Post-capture: basic image management.

In the misty hills of the Pa Hin Ngam National Park, Siam tulips *(Curcuma alismatifolia)* grow wild and amplify a tangible spiritual atmosphere.

ANDY FARRER

Finalist

The Path

The New Forest, Hampshire, England, UK

📷 Canon EOS 5DS, Canon 16-35mm lens, 4sec at f/11, ISO 100. Tripod, polarising filter, neutral density graduated filters. Post-capture: basic image management.

Dawn was breaking on Rockford Common in the New Forest and I was surrounded by the striking colours of sun-bronzed ferns and purple heather. This was perfectly complemented by the matching hues of morning light.

MONICA SIRI
FINALIST

Summer in the Sonoran Desert
Arizona, USA

Canon EOS 5D Mark III, Canon 24mm tilt-shift II lens, 3.2sec at f/20, ISO 100. Tripod, remote release. Post-capture: basic image management.

Despite extreme conditions, the Sonoran Desert is rich in plant life. The deep reds of sunset radiated beautifully from the translucent spines of cacti, stretching into the distance.

◄ DREW BUCKLEY

Highly Commended

Wild Garlic Sundown

National Trust Stackpole Estate, Pembrokeshire, Wales, UK

📷 Canon EOS 5D Mark IV, Canon 24-70mm lens, 1/5sec at f/16, ISO 100.
Tripod, neutral density graduated filter, circular polarising filter.
Post-capture: basic image management.

The last rays of light found their way past
the trees and onto the forest floor, which was
covered in a carpet of wild garlic *(Allium
ursinum)* flowers.

FRANCIS TAYLOR

Highly Commended

Hare's Tail Cotton Grass

Peak District National Park, Sheffield, England, UK

📷 Canon EOS 5D Mark III, Canon 16-35mm lens, 1/4000sec at f/11, ISO 100. Tripod.
Post-capture: basic image management.

A sea of flowering cotton grass *(Eriophorum vaginatum)*
stretches over the Ringinglow Moors in the Peak District
National Park. Cotton grass is a native, perennial sedge and in
early summer can be found covering desolate boggy areas of
moorland, easily recognised by its fluffy white seedheads.

ANNE MAENURM

Narcissus **Paradise**
Golica, Western Karawanks, Slovenia

📷 Canon EOS 5D Mark III, Canon 70-200mm lens, 1/3sec at f/20,
ISO 100. Tripod. Post-capture: basic image management.

By late May whole slopes on the peak of Golica are covered with wild *Narcissus* in full bloom, making for spectacular spring scenery.

TIANYI YU
HIGHLY COMMENDED

Slipper Orchid
Min Mountains, Sichuan Province, China

Canon EOS 5D Mark IV, Canon 16-35mm lens, 1/6sec at f/18, ISO 800. Post-capture: basic image management.

Cypripedium tibeticum has stunning richly coloured flowers ranging from maroon brown to purple. In the Min Mountains it can often be found growing around travertine limestone pools and waterfalls.

DAVE FIELDHOUSE
1st Place

Autumn in Padley Gorge
Peak District National Park, Derbyshire, England, UK

Canon EOS 5D Mark III, Canon 24-70mm lens, 1/90sec at f/8, ISO 1600. Post-capture: basic image management.

Padley Gorge is a honeypot location at this particular time of year, when photographers from all over the Peak District (and further afield) descend into its woodland glades. It took a while to find a composition I liked without anyone else in shot, but as the sun burnt away the last of the morning mist I achieved the image I was looking for.

MATTHEW HOLLAND
2ND PLACE

Dinorwig Pattern
Snowdonia National Park, Gwynedd, Wales, UK

📷 Nikon D500, Tamron 70-300mm macro lens, 1/30sec at f/8, ISO 100. Tripod. Post-capture: basic image management.

As we drove up to the disused Dinorwig Slate Quarry, the sun started to make an appearance. The light illuminated the blue and grey shades of slate and made the trees erupt with colour.

CHRIS DALE

3RD PLACE

Frostiest Tree in the Forest

Sherwood Forest, Nottinghamshire, England, UK

📷 Canon EOS 6D, Tamron 70-300mm macro lens, 1/50sec at f/5, ISO 200. Post-capture: basic image management.

This little frost-heavy sapling was captured at the very start of a long project exploring Sherwood Forest. Its dazzling form stood out in a small clearing surrounded by silver birch and bracken ferns.

DAVID MALIKOFF
FINALIST

Against the Fall
Wentworth Falls, Blue Mountains, New South Wales, Australia

Canon EOS 5D Mark III, Canon 24-105mm lens, 1/1000sec at f/4, ISO 320.
Post-capture: converted to black and white, added selective colour, basic image management.

I loved the tenacity of this little tree and the spirit it seemed to represent, holding on against the vast flow of water.
I selectively coloured the tree to emphasise this feeling.

◂ WILLIAM DORE

Finalist

The Last Stand

The Trossachs, Stirling, Scotland, UK

Nikon Df, Zeiss 135mm lens, 1/400sec at f/2.8, ISO 100. Post-capture: split tone effect added in Tonality Pro, basic image management.

An isolated group of pines, shrouded in mist and rain, stood defiant against the elements at Duke's Pass in the Trossachs.

EDWIG VANHASSEL

Finalist

The Last Leaves

High Fens Nature Reserve, Belgium

Canon EOS 5D Mark III, Canon 70-200mm lens, 1/125sec at f/16, ISO 800. Tripod. Post-capture: basic image management.

I waited for a day with early snow in the *Hautes Fagnes* so that I could combine and contrast its bleak purity with the final golden hues of autumn foliage.

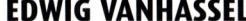

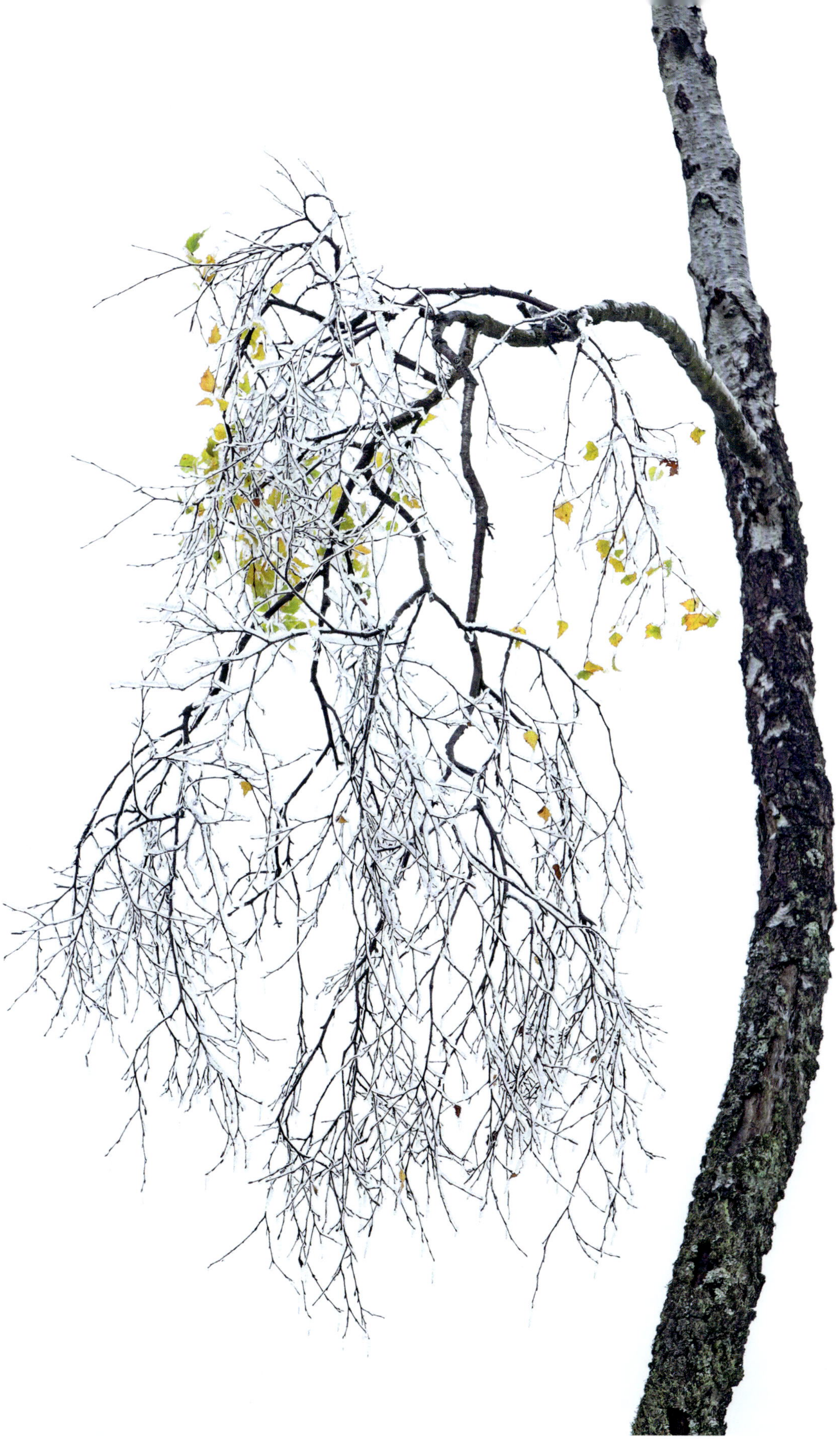

MARCIO CABRAL
FINALIST

Sucupira
São Domingos, Goiás, Brazil

📷 Canon EOS 5DS R, Nikkor 14mm lens, 25sec at
f/2.8, ISO 6400. Tripod, Fotodiox lens adapter,
Scurion 1200 lamp.
Post-capture: basic image management.

The *Pterodon emarginatus*, or
sucupira-branca in Portuguese,
is an endemic Brazilian tree of
the *Leguminosae* family, found
in the ecologically important
cerrado. I used a lamp at the
base of the tree to highlight its
form against the backdrop of the
Milky Way.

BRANDON YOSHIZAWA
Highly Commended

Into the Mist
Yosemite National Park, California, USA

Nikon D750, Nikkor 70-200mm lens, 1/30sec at f/16, ISO 1000. Tripod. Post-capture: basic image management.

The fog on this winter's day sat at the perfect height, ending just below the tips of the trees. I used my telephoto lens to make it look as if Bridalveil Fall poured into the sea of fog.

ANIL SUD
Highly Commended

Autumn in Patagonia
Patagonia, Argentina

📷 Canon EOS 5D Mark III, Canon 24-105mm lens, 6sec at f/14, ISO 50. Tripod. Post-capture: basic image management.

The waterfall added a fitting centrepiece to this blazing autumnal scene. The contrasting green vegetation emanated outwards into the burnt orange of the surrounding leaves.

ANDREA POZZI
1ST PLACE

Serendipity
Tombstone Territorial Park, Yukon Territory, Canada

Canon EOS 6D, Canon 16-35mm lens, 5sec at f/11, ISO 100. Tripod, neutral density graduated filter, polariser. Post-capture: basic image management.

I took this photograph whilst exploring the wilderness of the Yukon Territory; the landscape was awesome and truly wild. I sat down in the vegetation, took in the scenery and admired my surroundings – it was too beautiful to be real.

ESEN TUNAR
2ND PLACE

Mystic Glastonbury Tor
Shapwick Heath National Nature Reserve,
Glastonbury, England, UK

📷 Canon EOS 5D Mark II, Canon 70-200mm lens, 1/200sec at
f/13, ISO 100. Tripod. Post-capture: basic image management.

It was a beautiful misty spring morning at Shapwick Nature Reserve with Glastonbury Tor standing tall in the background.

CHRIS HERRING

3RD PLACE

Thornham Dawn
Norfolk, England, UK

Canon EOS 5DS, Canon 16-35mm lens, 1/10sec at f/16, ISO 400. Tripod, neutral density hard graduated filter. Post-capture: basic image management.

It was a peaceful and calming first light that illuminated the salt marshes at Thornham; the tranquillity was palpable.

ANDREA POZZI

Finalist

Autumnal Dream

Los Glaciares National Park, Patagonia, Argentina

📷 Canon EOS 6D, Canon 24-70mm lens, 0.3sec at f/11, ISO 200.
Tripod, neutral density graduated filter, polariser.
Post-capture: basic image management.

In the vast and primordial landscape of Patagonia, I was treated to the spectacle of a double rainbow to accompany the blazing colours of autumn. This park of outstanding natural beauty was awarded UNESCO World Heritage Site status in 1981.

FRANCIS TAYLOR

FINALIST

Roach End Barn

Peak District National Park, Staffordshire,
England, UK

📷 Canon EOS 5D Mark III, Canon 16-35mm lens,
0.5sec at f/8, ISO 100. Tripod.
Post-capture: basic image management.

When I reached the barn, I could see a
tiny gap under the cloud, so I sprinted
up the hill and set up my tripod. After
what felt like an age, the sun finally
dipped below the horizon and the sky
lit up with a stunning array of colour.

ADAM BURTON
FINALIST

Misty Blue Morning
Banff National Park, Alberta, Canada

📷 Nikon D800E, Nikkor 24-70mm lens, 0.8sec at f/11, ISO 100. Tripod,
neutral density graduated filter. Post-capture: basic image management.

It was an incredibly atmospheric morning in the Canadian
Rockies; Herbert Lake was like a mirror. However, I had
to wait a while for the mist to break in order to obtain the
gorgeous reflections of the mountains. The clouds then parted
just enough to reveal the very first light of a new day.

JULIAN ELLIOTT

HIGHLY COMMENDED

Spring in Val d'Orcia

Val d'Orcia, Tuscany, Italy

Canon EOS 6D, Canon 24mm tilt-shift lens, 1/13sec at f/11,
ISO 100. Tripod, cable release. Post-capture: basic image management.

The early dawn light helped lift the mist in Val d'Orcia, a UNESCO World Heritage Site. The backlit foreground poppies provided a perfect contrast to the endless green landscape.

MAURO TRONTO

HIGHLY COMMENDED

Devero

Alpe Veglia and Alpe Devero Natural Park, Piedmont, Italy

Canon EOS 5D Mark III, Canon 16-35mm lens, 1/6sec at f/16, ISO 100. Tripod, neutral density graduated filter. Post-capture: basic image management.

Val Buscagna is situated in the western region of the Alpe Devero park. For me, it is one of the most beautiful places in the whole of the Alps.

STEPHEN STUDD

Highly Commended

A View to Take Your Breath Away

Bagan, Myanmar

Canon EOS 6D, Canon 24-70mm lens, ISO 100. Tripod.
Post-capture: combined multiple images to form a panorama.

Numerous temple peaks punctuated the skyline above the trees on a misty morning before sunrise in Bagan. The city is a deeply mystical and spiritual place.

ANDREA POZZI

In the Frame

Los Glaciares National Park, Patagonia, Argentina

📷 Canon EOS 6D, Canon 16-35mm lens, 1sec at f/11, ISO 100.
Tripod, neutral density graduated filter, polariser.
Post-capture: basic image management.

I was walking amongst the stunning flora of Patagonia when I saw the granite peaks of *Cuernos del Paine* come into view. The scene was framed by the hard shapes of dead, twisted trees and the soft foreground textures of wild grasses.

JUSTIN MINNS
HIGHLY COMMENDED

Through the Mist
Halvergate Marshes, Norfolk, England, UK

Canon EOS 5D Mark IV, Canon 16-35mm lens, 3.2sec at f/16, ISO 100. Tripod, neutral density medium graduated filter. Post-capture: basic image management.

The summer sunrise began to clear the mist from the Broads, bringing an old drainage mill into view on the horizon. When the alarm goes off at 3am, I often wonder what on earth I am doing, but mornings like this make it all worthwhile.

◄ **CAROL CASSELDEN**
1ST PLACE

Through Icy Glass
Sussex, England, UK

📷 Nikon D7100, Nikkor 18-105mm lens, 1/50sec at f/5, ISO 160.
Post-capture: basic image management.

This photograph was taken one winter's morning after the hessian sacks had been removed from the glass frames of the greenhouse, but before the ice had completely melted and disappeared. The results of this freezing process were beautiful, unexpected and somewhat unique.

RAYMOND JONES
2ND PLACE

Golden Glow
Chirk, Denbighshire, Wales, UK

📷 Canon EOS 6D, Canon 100mm macro lens, 1/60sec at f/8, ISO 5000. Post-capture: basic image management.

If a shrub was rated on its ability to provide year-round beauty in both winter and summer then this *Hydrangea petiolaris* would be a contender for first prize.

CINDY VONDRAN

3RD PLACE

Exotic Swirl
Rockton, Illinois, USA

📷 Canon EOS 6D, Canon 100mm macro lens,
1/60sec at f/18, ISO 1250. Tripod.
Post-capture: added distortion in Adobe
Photoshop, basic image management.

After shooting this *Zantedeschia* (calla
lily) in my garden, I then manipulated
the image in Adobe Photoshop using
multiple layers and distortion to
showcase its beauty and structure.

STEPHEN MOORE

Finalist

Rainbow

Ness Botanic Gardens, Wirral, England, UK

📷 Canon EOS 500D, Canon 100mm macro lens, 1/125sec at f/5.6, ISO 100. Post-capture: basic image management.

In the lush undergrowth of Ness Botanic Gardens a full spectrum of colour was on display, offering a perfect photographic opportunity.

MINGHUI YUAN

FINALIST

Bubble Bath

Wuhan City, China

📷 Nikon D3S, Tamron 90mm macro lens, 1/125sec at f/18, ISO 800. Post-capture: basic image management.

In spring, when sunshine is sufficient, *Spirogyra* (a green algae) can produce large amounts of oxygen bubbles via photosynthesis. *Salvinia natans* (floating aquatic fern) then emerges and becomes the dominant plant by blocking sunlight to the algae below.

ULRIKE ADAM

Filigree Sea
Rhododendron-Park, Bremen, Germany

Canon EOS 70D, Canon 100mm macro lens, 1/2500sec at f/2.8, ISO 100. Post-capture: basic image management.

Early morning sunlight imparted a delicate and detailed filigree effect on this border of *Eryngium* (sea holly), highlighting the enchanting blue of the flowerheads.

JOCELYN HORSFALL
FINALIST

Impressionistic Ferns
RHS Wisley, Surrey, England, UK

📷 Fujifilm X-E2, Fujinon 55-200mm lens, 1/180sec at f/3.5, ISO 500. Tripod. Post-capture: added painterly effect using Topaz Labs software, basic image management.

Bright spring ferns in the glasshouse at RHS Wisley created a beautifully sweeping, natural canopy with graceful lines.

JOANNA SZPAK OSTACHOWSKA ▶
FINALIST

Weeds
Warsaw, Poland

📷 Nikon D750, Tokina 100mm macro lens, 1/100sec at f/22, ISO 5600. Post-capture: basic image management.

I am fascinated by the small, inconspicuous lives of some plants. When studied closely they communicate a delicacy and fragility that has to be captured.

JACKY PARKER ►
HIGHLY COMMENDED

Spring *Magnolia*
Iver, Buckinghamshire, England, UK

📷 Nikon D750, Nikkor 105mm macro lens, 1/200sec at f/5.6, ISO 200.
Post-capture: combined and edited two images, basic image management.

I combined two images of the same *Magnolia* in Adobe Photoshop and adjusted opacity settings of the layers to give the illusion of movement.

JACKIE KRAMER ►
HIGHLY COMMENDED

Nigella Queen
Victoria, British Columbia, Canada

📷 Canon EOS 5D Mark III, Canon 100mm macro lens, 1/800sec at f/4, ISO 400.
Post-capture: basic image management.

I captured this *Nigella* flower with a seedpod in the background to create an interesting and alluring composition. For me, the flower is a real treasure.

◄ NICKY FLINT
1st Place

Through the Garden
Great Dixter House & Gardens, East Sussex, England, UK

📷 Canon EOS 450D, Canon 17-55mm lens, 1/160sec at f/8, ISO 200.
Post-capture: basic image management.

On my visit to Great Dixter, the family home of gardener and gardening writer Christopher Lloyd, the morning light in the High Garden was simply enchanting. A gentle mist softened the light and created a magical atmosphere where heavy dew glistened on filigree fennel and backlit *Allium* flowers enticed me deeper and deeper into the garden beyond.

JOHN GLOVER
2nd Place

Merriments
East Sussex, England, UK

📷 Nikon D3X, Nikkor 24-70mm lens, 1/10sec at f/11, ISO 100. Tripod.
Post-capture: basic image management.

As the sun was rising over this late summer border at Merriments Garden and Nursery, one could almost feel the warmth and energy of the season now reach its zenith.

JOHN GLOVER
3RD PLACE

Midwinter
Great Dixter House & Gardens, East Sussex, England, UK

📷 Nikon D3X, Nikkor 24-70mm lens, 1/250sec at f/13, ISO 100. Tripod.
Post-capture: basic image management.

Midwinter still holds many opportunities for the
garden photographer. The cold air and position
of the sun can create magical diffused light,
exposing a hidden seasonal beauty.

JOE WAINWRIGHT

FINALIST

High Summer

Bluebell Cottage Gardens, Cheshire, England, UK

📷 Canon EOS 5D Mark II, Canon 24-70mm lens, 1/100sec at f/13, ISO 800.
Tripod. Post-capture: basic image management.

A lush summer border at Bluebell Cottage Gardens was illuminated by the promising light of a July morning.

NIGEL MCCALL
FINALIST

The Jubilee Woodland Garden

Aberglasney House and Gardens, Carmarthenshire, Wales, UK

📷 Canon EOS 5DS R, Canon 24-105mm lens, 0.3sec at f/16, ISO 100. Tripod, remote release.
Post-capture: basic image management.

In spring and early summer the Jubilee Woodland Garden is a very atmospheric place to visit – especially in early morning light. It is a woodland bog garden with a natural but exotic feel, displaying a combination of *Zantedeschia aethiopica*, *Iris*, candelabra *Primula* and giant *Gunnera* leaves.

ANNIE GREEN-ARMYTAGE
FINALIST

Sunrise at Dale Farm
Dereham, Norfolk, England, UK

📷 Canon EOS 6D, Canon 24-70mm lens, 1/25sec at f/20, ISO 250. Tripod, filters.
Post-capture: basic image management.

Tucked away behind a hedge, next to a busy road, close to the centre of the town, the garden at Dale Farm is dominated by its magnificent pond. The glorious yellow of sunrise was amplified by *Inula magnifica* and *Lysimachia ciliata* 'Firecracker'.

MARIANNE MAJERUS

Morning Has Broken

The National Trust Coughton Court,
Warwickshire, England, UK

📷 Canon EOS 5D Mark III, Canon 24-70mm lens, 1/15sec at f/16,
ISO 400. Tripod. Post-capture: basic image management.

Morning had broken at Coughton
Court's Walled Garden and the carefully
choreographed colour of the border
looked beautiful in the shadow of St.
Peter's Church.

ANNIE GREEN-ARMYTAGE
Highly Commended

The Moon Gate

Schlosspark Dennenlohe, Bavaria, Germany

Canon EOS 6D, Canon 24-70mm lens, 1/8sec at f/16, ISO 400.
Tripod, filters. Post-capture: basic image management.

The Moon Gate connects the Private Garden with the *Rhododendron* Park, inviting you to travel into another world with carefully selected Asian specimens, such as the *Cornus controversa* 'Variegata' just beyond the entrance.

JOE WAINWRIGHT
Highly Commended

Trentham Gardens
Staffordshire, England, UK

Canon EOS 5D Mark II, Canon 24-70mm lens, 1sec at f/16, ISO 100. Tripod. Post-capture: basic image management.

As I took this photograph, a magical January frost was sparkling on the borders of the Italian Garden at Trentham.

JASON INGRAM

The Wind Garden

Folly Farm, Berkshire, England, UK

Nikon D3X, Nikkor 24-70mm lens, 1/8sec at f/16, ISO 100. Tripod. Post-capture: basic image management.

Early morning sunlight shone through the canopy of an oak tree overlooking the wind garden at Folly Farm, highlighting the tips of the ornamental grasses.

NIGEL MCCALL
1ST PLACE

Morning Mist and Mellow Fruitfulness
Aberglasney Gardens, Carmarthenshire, Wales, UK

Canon EOS 5DS R, Canon 24-105mm lens, 1/15sec at f/11, ISO 100. Tripod, remote release. Post-capture: basic image management.

In the warm, heavy mist of an August morning the Kitchen Garden at Aberglasney had a delightfully romantic atmosphere. Here, heritage fruit, cut flowers, vegetables and herbs are grown side by side and arranged by colour, making the garden a joy to photograph throughout much of the year.

SHAOFENG ZHANG

2ND PLACE

A Good Harvest is in Sight
Lishui, Zhejiang Province, China

📷 Nikon D5, Nikkor 24-70mm lens, 30sec at f/11, ISO 50. Tripod.

The Meiyuan Terrace has an agricultural history stretching back at least 1,000 years. The landscape of rolling hills and golden rice also attracts tourists to the area, yielding another kind of harvest time treasure.

SUWANDI CHANDRA

3RD PLACE

The Cinnamon Farmer

Flores, Indonesia

📷 Pentax K-3, Pentax 16-50mm lens, 1/60sec at f/8, ISO 100.
Post-capture: basic image management.

After collecting cinnamon from the forest, this farmer left the rolls of bark to dry in the sun in preparation for sale at a nearby market.

ANIL SUD

FINALIST

Morning Fog
Haridwar, Uttarakhand, India

Canon EOS 5D Mark III, Canon 70-200mm lens, 1/200sec at f/8, ISO 3200. Post-capture: basic image management.

As the morning fog begun to clear, a rice farmer checked over the irrigation of the paddies, ensuring a continual and smooth flow of water.

HANS VAN HORSSEN
FINALIST

Apple Blossom
Haaften, The Netherlands

📷 Canon EOS 6D, Canon 70-200mm lens, 1/1000sec at f/8, ISO 640.
Post-capture: basic image management.

The apple harvest this year was excellent and this photograph explains why. Success depends on protecting the delicate apple blossom from late night frost.

FLAVIO CATALANO
Finalist

Summer Treasures
Turin, Italy

Nikon D750, Nikkor 24-120mm lens, 1/10sec at f/4, ISO 100. Tripod. Post-capture: basic image management.

Tomatoes are perhaps the most widespread vegetable in Italy. We like to think of them as the transmutation of the sun itself. Their round form and fiery colour make them look like precious jewels.

JASON INGRAM

Kasteel Kitchen Garden

Kasteel Hex, Heers, Belgium

Nikon D3X, Nikkor 24-70mm lens, 1/6sec at f/16, ISO 100.
Tripod. Post-capture: basic image management.

Rows of verdant crops became illuminated by the first rays of morning sun.

GLORIA KING

HIGHLY COMMENDED

Lotus Cultivation

Loikaw, Kayah State, Myanmar

📷 Sony NEX-7, Sony 18-55mm lens, 1/200sec at f/16, ISO 200.
Post-capture: basic image management.

I came across this area whilst hiking in the Loikaw area during autumn. The lotus *(Nelumbo)* leaves were displaying striking seasonal colours whilst the stems created interesting patterns in the water.

ANNIE GREEN-ARMYTAGE
1st Place

City Campus
Hong Kong, China

📷 Fujifilm X-T2, Fujinon 18-55mm lens, 1/30sec at f/20, ISO 250.
Post-capture: basic image management.

This green space is on the edge of the Mong Kwok Ping Garden which sits in a compact area between buildings belonging to The University of Hong Kong. Hong Kong is one of the most densely populated cities on the planet, so green space is essential in order to promote health and well-being.

VANDA RALEVSKA
2ND PLACE

Autumnal City Morning
London, England, UK

📷 Fujifilm X-T2, Fujinon 18-135mm lens, 1/8sec at f/16, ISO 200. Tripod.
Post-capture: basic image management.

It was one of those autumnal mornings when a heavy fog rolled on to the streets of London and transformed the city into a soft, ever-evolving painting.

YINGTING SHIH

3rd Place

Self-Reflection

Taichung City, Taiwan

📷 Canon EOS 7D Mark II, Tamron 16-300mm macro lens, 1/250sec at f/8, ISO 100.
Post-capture: basic image management.

Trees in urban environments can provide a shelter from the noise and pace of modernity and give us a chance for self-reflection – in nature, one can always see oneself more clearly.

IRINA LOGRA

FINALIST

Custodians of Light

Venice, Los Angeles, California, USA

📷 Canon EOS 5D Mark II, Canon 50mm lens, 25sec at f/9, ISO 100.
Post-capture: basic image management.

The Venice Canals are a green, peaceful hideaway from the otherwise busy urban centres nearby. It was perhaps the advent of the Great Depression that prevented all of the canals from being filled in, so the public can still enjoy the tranquillity they have to offer.

ANNIE GREEN-ARMYTAGE
FINALIST

Dolores Park
Mission Dolores Park, San Francisco, USA

Canon EOS 6D, Canon 24-70mm lens, 1/30sec at f/13, ISO 800.
Filters. Post-capture: basic image management.

The sun was setting over the city as I stood at the top of Mission Dolores Park, which is one of San Francisco's most popular destinations and the vibrant heart of a culturally diverse neighbourhood. The park encompasses nearly 16 acres and has Leave No Trace™ status.

ANIL SUD

Autumn Colour

Michigan, USA

Canon EOS 5D Mark II, Canon 70-200mm lens, 1/100sec at f/2.8, ISO 100. Tripod. Post-capture: basic image management.

Framed through the window of an old derelict building I saw the colours of autumn beyond and the enduring strength of natural processes.

VICKY SCOTT

From the Sky
Corfu Town, Corfu, Greece

Canon EOS 550D, Canon 50mm lens, 1/4000sec at f/2.5, ISO 100. Post-capture: basic image management.

Corfu Town is surrounded by an ancient green landscape that has coexisted with human settlements for thousands of years. Corfu's Old Town has been listed as a UNESCO World Heritage Site since 2007.

MATTEO CARASSALE

Vertical Forest

Bosco Verticale, Milan, Italy

📷 Canon EOS 5D Mark III, Canon 70-200mm lens, 1/500sec at f/9, ISO 800.
　Post-capture: basic image management.

As cities face the growing problem of air pollution a new green spirit is being championed in architecture. This building, designed by Stefano Boeri, incorporates trees into the construction and is equivalent to a small forest.

MATTEO CARASSALE ▶

Green in Place

Milan, Italy

📷 Canon EOS 5D Mark III, Canon 24mm tilt-shift lens, 1/40sec at f/11, ISO 200.
　Post-capture: basic image management.

The Piazza del Duomo in Milan is not only admired for its architecture but also a new green square, featuring banana plants, palms *(Trachycarpus fortunei)*, shrubs, grasses and perennials.

◀ ALAN PRICE
1st Place

Female Blackbird
Criccieth, Gwynedd, Wales, UK

📷 Nikon D7100, Nikon 300mm lens, 1/1250sec at f/6.3, ISO 3200.
Post-capture: basic image management.

This female blackbird was on her way back to the nest to supplement its construction with fresh vegetation.

PETAR SABOL
2nd Place

Fairy Tale
Palovec, Croatia

📷 Sony α99, Meyer Optik Görlitz Trioplan 100mm macro lens, 1/60sec at f/2.8, ISO 50. Tripod.
Post-capture: basic image management.

This really was a once in a lifetime photograph. In a forest near my town I came across this unbelievable scene of insect behaviour. I used an old vintage lens to achieve the bokeh, but had to work fast as the light was quickly disappearing and the opportunity would be gone forever.

JONATHAN NEED

Goldfinch

Snowdonia National Park, Wales, UK

📷 Nikon D3S, Sigma 300mm lens, 1/4000sec at f/4,
ISO 800. Tripod. Post-capture: basic image management.

The metallic bronze leaves of an autumn beech tree perfectly complemented the colours of this perching goldfinch.

HANS VAN HORSSEN

Finalist

Nursery Web

Jistrum, Friesland, The Netherlands

Canon EOS 6D, Canon 70-200mm lens, 1/800sec at f/6.3, ISO 640. Post-capture: basic image management.

The nursery web spider constructs webs for protecting their young, not for hunting. This female chose a *Helenium* flower as a suitable foundation.

RIPAN BISWAS

FINALIST

Guide to the Galaxy
Cooch Behar, West Bengal, India

📷 Nikon D750, Laowa 15mm macro lens, 30sec at f/4, ISO 2000. Tripod, flash.
Post-capture: combined two exposures together, basic image management.

I saw this meditative frog sitting on the leaf of a water hyacinth, peering up at the Milky Way. I approached silently and made two 30 second exposures to ensure good light on both the frog and night sky.

INÊS LEONARDO
FINALIST

On Top of the World
Serra da Arrábida Natural Park,
Setúbal, Portugal

📷 Canon EOS 60D, Canon 100mm macro lens, 1/750sec at
   f/2.8, ISO 400. Post-capture: basic image management.

A small butterfly landed on a
flowerhead just ahead of me as I was
walking and I approached slowly
for the shot. I chose this particular
composition as the butterfly was
facing sideways, yet centred on the
flower, giving a sense of balance.

◄ WEI FU
FINALIST

I See You
King Rama IX Park, Bangkok, Thailand

📷 Canon EOS 5D Mark IV, Canon 100-400mm lens,
   1/800sec at f/5.6, ISO 1600.
   Post-capture: basic image management.

I saw this sunbird staring at me
through the undergrowth, naturally
framed by two stems in the
foreground and using an unopened
flower bud as a makeshift perch.

RADIM SCHREIBER

A Flash of Hope

Fairfield, Iowa, USA

📷 Sony α7S II, Canon 100mm macro lens, 1/15sec at f/2.8,
ISO 12800. Post-capture: basic image management.

I have been waiting to take a photograph like this for a long time, then it finally happened. I pressed the shutter release just as the firefly's bioluminescence lit up the surrounding flowers.

THOMAS DELAHAYE

Highly Commended

Sweet Robin
Boucieu-le-Roi, France

📷 Canon EOS 5D Mark III, Canon 500mm lens, 1/1600sec at f/5.6, ISO 1250. Post-capture: basic image management.

My mother's house in the south of France created a perfect backdrop to capture the character of this European robin.

MINGHUI YUAN
HIGHLY COMMENDED

The Dance of Radiant Light
Wuhan City, China

📷 Nikon D3S, Tamron 90mm macro lens, 1/80sec at f/16, ISO 400.
Post-capture: basic image management.

After the rain came to Wuhan, the air temperature began to increase as the sun came out, encouraging this frog to bask on a palm leaf. The centre of the palm and its radiating fronds mirror this natural process.

◄ **CATHRYN BALDOCK**
1ST PLACE

Lily Pads
Northumberland, England, UK

📷 Canon EOS 5D Mark II, Canon 24-105mm lens, 1/60sec
at f/9, ISO 100. Post-capture: manipulated and overlaid
multiple images, basic image management.

I overlaid multiple images of lily pads
at different scales to emphasise their
beauty and intricacy.

RON TEAR
2ND PLACE

Afterlife of Plants
Royal Botanic Gardens, Kew,
London, England, UK

📷 Canon EOS 5D Mark III, Canon 100-400mm lens,
1/5000sec at f/4.5, ISO 1600.
Post-capture: basic image management.

As the last rays of light shone
through the Palm House, I noticed
these shapes appear on the glass, like
ancient botanical fossils waiting to be
discovered.

◄ GREG VIVASH
3RD PLACE

Floral Dreams
Arundel, West Sussex, England, UK

📷 Canon EOS 6D, Canon 16-35mm lens, 1/250sec at f/10, ISO 200.
   Post-capture: blended together multiple images, basic image management.

I blended together multiple images of poppies,
daffodils and lavender to create a floral dreamscape
with painterly qualities.

BOB LUIJKS
FINALIST

Birch
Vaals, The Netherlands

📷 Canon EOS 5D Mark III, Canon 70-200mm lens, 1/6sec at f/2.8, ISO 800.
   In-camera multiple exposures. Tripod. Post-capture: basic image management.

In order to fully express the explosion of autumn
colours I used the multiple exposure function on my
camera to create layers of intrigue and beauty.

DAVID JORDAN
FINALIST

Trapped
Norwich, Norfolk, England, UK

📷 Canon EOS M3, body cap pinhole, 1/20sec at f/180, ISO 1600.
Post-capture: basic image management.

This photograph was taken using a body cap pinhole in place of a normal lens. This uses a 0.02mm hole giving an effective aperture of f/180. The images that it creates lack absolute sharpness, but they have an interesting tone and texture which amplify the mood of the capture.

CATHRYN BALDOCK ▶
FINALIST

Azaleas
Exbury Gardens, Hampshire, England, UK

📷 Canon EOS 5D Mark III, Canon 24-105mm lens, 1/5sec at f/10, ISO 100.
Post-capture: basic image management.

I used intentional camera movement to create an abstraction of *Azalea* in flower.

◄ **HELEN STORER**
FINALIST

Temple Hill
The National Trust Sheringham Park,
Norfolk, England, UK

📷 Canon EOS 5D Mark III, Canon 16-35mm lens, 1/50sec
at f/10, ISO 100. In-camera multiple exposures,
average setting. Post-capture: basic image management.

Standing resplendent above
Sheringham Hall, the view from
the temple at Sheringham Park is
breathtaking. Wander through the
grounds and you will discover why
Sheringham became the personal
favourite of its designer, Humphry
Repton.

FRANTISEK RERUCHA
HIGHLY COMMENDED

Pasqueflower
Czech Republic

📷 Canon EOS 70D, Canon 60mm macro lens,
1/5sec at f/14, ISO 200. Tripod.
Post-capture: digitally created layered composition.

I find dry flowers have a real and
lasting beauty. The star of this
dried flower composition is the
pasqueflower, which takes centre stage
with vibrant dark purple petals.

GIUSEPPE SATRIANI
HIGHLY COMMENDED

Lake of the Arboreal Swans
Salamanca, Spain

📷 Panasonic Lumix DMC-G2, Lumix 45-200mm lens, 1/160sec at f/11, ISO 200. Post-capture: added mirroring effect.

For this ethereal image, even though the symmetry was added post-capture, I only needed a few simple ingredients for the composition: frost, fog, air and pine.

◄ JOCELYN HORSFALL
HIGHLY COMMENDED

Crocosmia Abstraction
London, England, UK

📷 Nikon FM2, Tamron 90mm macro lens, 1/125sec at f/2.8, ISO 25. Tripod, studio lights. Post-capture: scanned negative, basic image management.

By selecting an extremely shallow depth of field and shooting through a textured glass vase I was able to create this abstract, impressionistic image.

ANDREW GEORGE
HIGHLY COMMENDED

Thunder
Río Tinto, Andalucía, Spain

📷 Nikon D810, Nikkor 24-70mm lens, 0.4sec at f/16, ISO 100. Tripod. Post-capture: basic image management.

The Río Tinto is famed for its coloration due to thousands of years of mining in the surrounding areas. The reflections of trees make us pause for thought as we examine the impact of human activity on the environment.

CLARE FORBES
1ST PLACE

Sunrise at Ellicar
Doncaster, England, UK

📷 Canon EOS 5D Mark II, Canon 24-105mm lens, 1/30sec at f/16, ISO 250. Tripod.
Post-capture: basic image management.

The first rays of morning sunlight caught the remnants of mist hanging over the natural swimming pool at Ellicar Gardens. After a heavy dew, the grasses surrounding the pool were laden with sparkling water droplets.

ANNIE GREEN-ARMYTAGE
2ND PLACE

Sunrise at the Summerhouse
Chapel Cottage, Norfolk, England, UK

📷 Canon EOS 6D, Canon 24-70mm lens, 1/6sec at f/18, ISO 400.
Tripod, filters. Post-capture: basic image management.

This summerhouse is one of Sarah Butler's favourite spots in her garden at Chapel Cottage. Here she sits and takes time out to watch dragonflies and other insects swooping over the pond.

DANIÈLE DUGRÉ

3RD PLACE

A Place to Dream

Schlosspark Dennenlohe, Bavaria, Germany

Nikon D600, Nikkor 24-120mm lens, 1/125sec at f/11, ISO 125. Tripod, polarising filter. Post-capture: basic image management.

Even though the grounds of the estate are extensive, there are lots of hidden places to discover, where one can sit and enjoy being amongst nature.

JAKE TURNER   **Colour Palette,** Wildflower Landscapes

ANDY FARRER   **Pink Sunrise,** Wildflower Landscapes

STEPHANIE FOOTE   **Skomer,** Wildflower Landscapes

ANDREA HERIBANOVA
Icelandic Lupins, Wildflower Landscapes

FRANCIS TAYLOR
Lawrence Field in Bloom, Wildflower Landscapes

ANNE MAENURM   **Summer Fields,** Wildflower Landscapes

DREW BUCKLEY   **Thrift,** Wildflower Landscapes

MARK GRAY   **Tidal Guardians,** Trees, Woods & Forests

IGNACIO HERAS   **Alone,** Trees, Woods & Forests

FRANCIS DOST   **Breathe the Forests,** Trees, Woods & Forests

ANIL SUD   **Silhouette,** Trees, Woods & Forests

ANIL SUD
Tree in Fog, Trees, Woods & Forests

ULRIKE ADAM
Winter Tree, Trees, Woods & Forests

J. K. PUTNAM
The Bowl at Sunrise, Breathing Spaces

DANIÈLE DUGRÉ   **Through the Lens of Monet,** Trees, Woods & Forests

DANIÈLE DUGRÉ   **Sunrise over the Sinn River,** Breathing Spaces

FRANCIS TAYLOR   **Fairbrook Falls,** *Breathing Spaces*

ALAN BEVIS   **Early Morning by the Lake,** *Breathing Spaces*

LIJUNWANG WANG   **Hometown Fog,** *Breathing Spaces*

MARIANNE MAJERUS   **Restful Place,** *Breathing Spaces*

ANNE NEIWAND   **Hope Springs Eternal,** *Breathing Spaces*

MARK BAUER
A Carpet of Colour, Breathing Spaces

NIGEL BURKITT　　　　　　　　　　　　　　*Persicaria* **Plumes,** The Beauty of Plants

JACKIE KRAMER　　　　　　　　　　**Queen Anne's Lace,** The Beauty of Plants

J. K. PUTNAM
Algae Landscape, Breathing Spaces

ALEKSANDER IVANOV
Solar, The Beauty of Plants

YI FAN
Concomitance, The Beauty of Plants

MINGHUI YUAN
Holding On, The Beauty of Plants

JACKIE KRAMER
Dancing *Paphiopedilum*, The Beauty of Plants

JACKY PARKER
***Hydrangea paniculata* 'Unique',** The Beauty of Plants

YANG NIU   **Orchid Under the Prayer Flags,** The Beauty of Plants

MARIANNE MAJERUS   **Borrowed Landscape,** Beautiful Gardens

BARRY EDGE   *Echinops,* The Beauty of Plants

JENNIFER GUYTON   **The Ancient One,** The Beauty of Plants

JOE WAINWRIGHT **The *Dahlia* Walk in September,** Beautiful Gardens

CAROL CASSELDEN **The Peacock Garden,** Beautiful Gardens

VOLKER MICHAEL **Springtime in Hermannshof,** Beautiful Gardens

JASON INGRAM **Hauser & Wirth Garden,** Beautiful Gardens

RICHARD MURPHY **Framing the View,** Beautiful Gardens

JUDE GADD **The Kitchen Garden,** The Bountiful Earth

JULIAN ELLIOTT **Village of Plenty,** The Bountiful Earth

SIYUAN MA **The Green Corridor,** Greening The City

MEHRNAZ DARGAHIFAR **Water Lilies,** Greening The City

ANNIE GREEN-ARMYTAGE **Green Oasis,** Greening The City

HENRIK SPRANZ

Early Dinner, Wildlife in the Garden

TONYA WILHELM
Caterpillar Feet, Wildlife in the Garden

LEIGH AYRES

Meadowhawk, Wildlife in the Garden

MINGHUI YUAN
Mohican Caterpillar, Wildlife in the Garden

HENRIK SPRANZ
Alpine Paradise, Wildlife in the Garden

SALLY KILPIN   **All Eyes on Me,** Wildlife in the Garden

AMANDA WRIGHT
Gladiolus **Green Grid,** Abstract Views

MATTEO CARASSALE   **Italian Love,** Wildlife in the Garden

DAVID NICHOLAS DAVIES   **Summer Evening,** Abstract Views

ROBIN CARLSON
Moonset, Abstract Views

JOCELYN HORSFALL
Painterly *Freesia*, Abstract Views

ANNEMARIE FARLEY **Tulip Abstract,** Abstract Views

KIMBERLY GUST **Golden Girl,** Abstract Views

CAROLYNE BARBER **A Touch of Japan,** Abstract Views

YOUNG GARDEN
PHOTOGRAPHER
OF THE YEAR

YANG YU WEI

YANG YU WEI

1ST PLACE

Hydrangea

Palo Alto, California, USA

📷 Canon EOS 5D Mark IV, Canon 100mm macro lens, 1/100sec at f/3.5, ISO 800. Tripod.
Post-capture: basic image management.

It was a beautiful sunny morning when I visited this garden with my family. I managed to capture this *Hydrangea* with a dazzling background bokeh as light shone through the tree canopy.

YANG YU WEI
2ND PLACE

Dandelion
Almaden Valley, San Jose, California, USA

📷 Canon EOS 5D Mark IV, Canon 100mm macro lens, 1/80sec at f/7.1, ISO 640. Tripod. Post-capture: basic image management.

I bought a huge dandelion from the florist and captured it in front of a pear tree for an interesting background, creating an enchanting composition.

WILL JENKINS
3RD PLACE

Crop Art
Inverness, Scotland, UK

📷 DJI Mavic Pro Drone, 1/50sec at f/2.2, ISO 103. Apple iPhone, neutral density graduated filter.

This photograph was part of a project where I was looking at how aerial views of fields can look like paintings. Hovering over these spaces was fascinating – I would just watch the crops sway from side to side as I waited for the right composition.

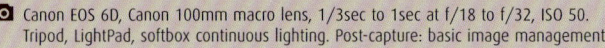

MANDY DISHER

THE ROYAL PHOTOGRAPHIC SOCIETY GOLD MEDAL

1st Place, The Beauty of Plants

Simple Nature

Cambridgeshire, England, UK

Canon EOS 6D, Canon 100mm macro lens, 1/3sec to 1sec at f/18 to f/32, ISO 50.
Tripod, LightPad, softbox continuous lighting. Post-capture: basic image management.

THE **RPS**

ROYAL
PHOTOGRAPHIC
SOCIETY

From early spring to late summer I chose a number of white flowers to photograph, selecting each for its unique qualities and individual characteristics. I wanted to express simplicity, happiness and well-being by using a high-key technique. In this way, I was able to capture the pure, simple and natural beauty of each plant. These included: *Alstroemeria, Convallaria, Leucanthemum, Cosmos, Galanthus* and *Tulipa*.

STEVE LOWRY

THE ROYAL PHOTOGRAPHIC SOCIETY SILVER MEDAL

2ND PLACE, TREES, WOODS & FORESTS

The Heart of the Woods

Portstewart, Northern Ireland, UK

📷 Olympus D70 microscope digital camera, microscope objective lens,
1/60sec to 1/13sec, ISO 100. Olympus BX45 microscope, polarising filters,
wave retarding filters. Post-capture: basic image management.

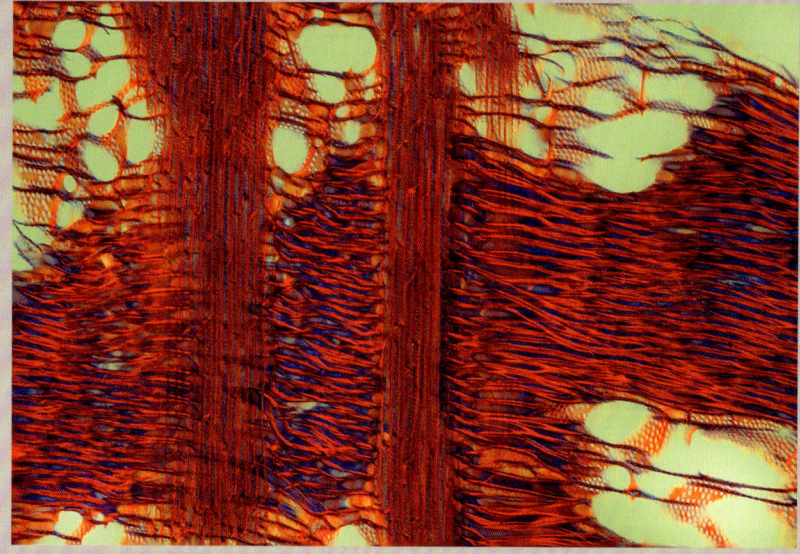

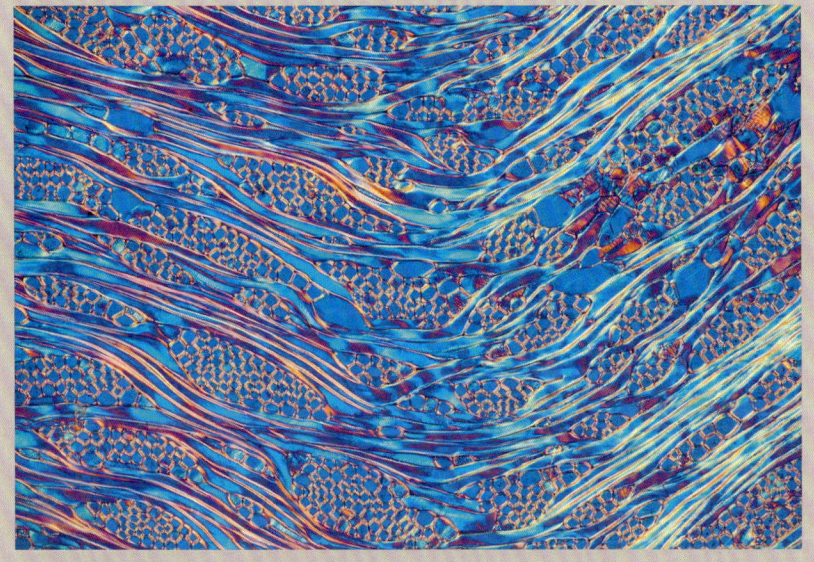

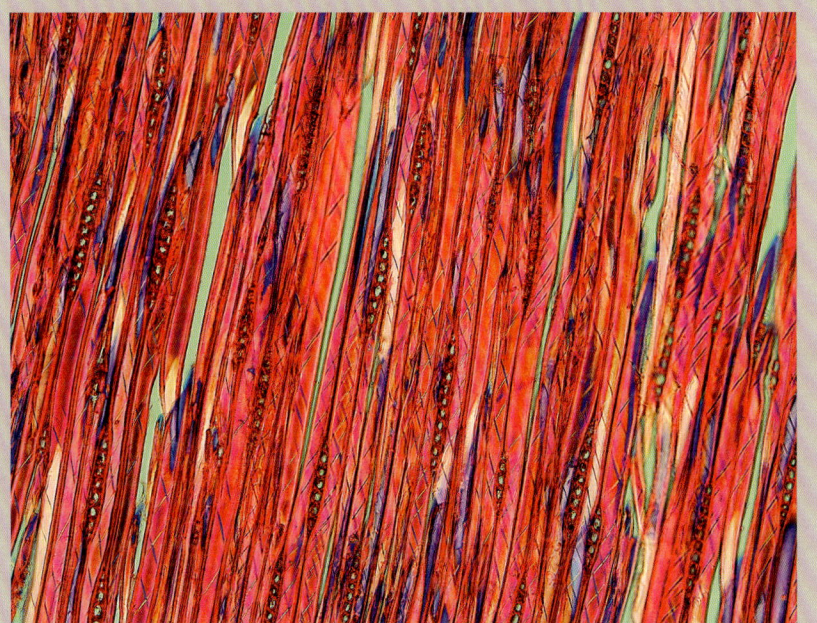

For over 150 years polarised light microscopy has been used in the examination of the structure of wood. For my portfolio, I have used polarised light and wave retarding filters to produce images of a range of tree species, chosen for their aesthetic appeal. These species included: *Larix, Pinus sylvestris, Sassafras, Ulmus minor, Pseudotsuga taxifolia* and *Cedrus libani.*

HONG ZHAO
THE ROYAL PHOTOGRAPHIC SOCIETY BRONZE MEDAL
3RD PLACE, ABSTRACT VIEWS

Water Lilies & Lotus
Guyi Garden, Nanxiang, Shanghai, China

📷 Nikon D700, Nikkor 105mm macro lens, 1/100sec to 1/60sec at f/11, ISO 250. Post-capture: added painterly quality.

The water lilies at Guyi garden in Shanghai were in full bloom when I visited in the summer. The scene is always so beautiful and reminds one of a Monet painting. I wanted to recreate this and set about capturing photographs that were reminiscent of his oil paintings.

PIERRE PELLEGRINI
FINALIST, BLACK & WHITE

In the Enchanted Forest
Ticino, Switzerland

📷 Hasselblad 503CW + Phase One P20+, Hasselblad 40mm lens, 1/239sec to 1sec at f/11 to f/16, ISO 100. Tripod, neutral density graduated filter.
Post-capture: converted to black and white, basic image management.

Even after I visited this enchanted forest I can still smell the scent of the leaves and hear the sound they made underfoot; I still feel the cold of the fog and rain; I still feel the magical atmosphere; I still remember the feeling of being completely alone with nature.

VALERIE DENNISON

FINALIST, MY GARDEN STORIES

The Garden That Came in From the Cold

County Limerick, Republic of Ireland

📷 Canon EOS 5D Mark III, Canon 24-105mm lens, 1/160sec to 1/6sec at f/4 to f/16, ISO 250 to ISO 500. Tripod, remote release. Post-capture: basic image management.

We lost our wonderful garden to the bitter freeze of December 2010 – January 2011. Very little survived the temperature of -12°C which lasted for a fortnight and never rose above freezing point. This story is about the complete demoralisation my husband and I suffered from the destruction of our garden. We subsequently neglected the garden for seven years, allowing it to take care of itself, which it did with ferocity. Then, tentatively, in the spring of 2017, we made an effort to start again.

CLAY BOLT

HIGHLY COMMENDED, WILDLIFE IN THE GARDEN

Bees at Work

South Dakota, Montana, Wisconsin, South Carolina, California, USA

📷 Nikon D300 + D600 + D750, Sigma 15mm fisheye lens, Sigma 180mm macro lens,
1/1600sec to 1/25sec at f/9 to f/16, ISO 400 to ISO 2000. Post-capture: basic image management.

The United States and Canada are home to approximately 4,000 species of native bees, which perform an incredible range of pollination activities. They can be found on high mountain peaks, to dry desert landscapes and snow-covered fields. Unfortunately, many of North America's native bees are suffering under the pressures of development, chemical threats, and introduced disease. I believe that it is important for viewers to connect with both the bees and the habitat they help to support.

MASUMI SHIOHARA
HIGHLY COMMENDED, STILL LIFE

Fruits
Shiojiri, Japan

📷 Pentax 645 Z + Canon EOS 5D Mark II, Canon 45mm tilt-shift lens, Canon 100mm macro lens, 1.6sec to 3.2sec at f/9 to f/18, ISO 400 to ISO 500. Post-capture: added textured backgrounds.

As an orchardist, I have endeavoured to create an artistic record of fruit that I have grown at its most visually beautiful form prior to being harvested. My artwork is similar to classic botanical drawings in the sense that I seek to depict a precise level of detail whilst at the same time attempt to communicate their aesthetic beauty. Specimens included varieties of: *Vitis*, *Prunus*, *Pyrus* and *Malus*.

HANS VAN HORSSEN
HIGHLY COMMENDED, BREATHING SPACES

Sunrise on the Dutch Polders
De Betuwe, Gelderland, The Netherlands

📷 Canon EOS 40D + 6D, Canon 70-200mm lens, 1/3200sec to 1/500sec at f/5.6 to f/7.1, ISO 100 to ISO 640. Tripod. Post-capture: basic image management.

As a garden designer, I take a lot of inspiration from nature and these early morning scenes were magnificent. The themes of peace, stillness and silent beauty run through this portfolio, all brought together by the wordless interactions of horses, birds and an ever-present mist.

MICHAEL HUDSON
1st Place

Ancient Oak Tree
Tŷ Canol Woods, Pembrokeshire, Wales, UK

📷 Canon EOS 5D Mark II, Canon 16-35mm lens, 1/80sec at f/7.1, ISO 100. Tripod.
Post-capture: basic image management.

I shot this ancient oak using a (converted) infrared camera. It stands guard at the entrance to the Tŷ Canol Woods in south-west Wales.

LOTTE GRØNKJÆR-FUNCH
2ND PLACE

Twice the Same
Copenhagen, Denmark

📷 Nikon D610, Nikkor 105mm lens, 1/160sec at f/5.6, ISO 50.
Post-capture: created a copy of one flower, basic image management.

I have had tulips growing in my garden for the past 25 years and this was the very first of the year. It has excellent symmetry and is very photogenic.

MARCIO CABRAL
3RD PLACE

Cerrado Sunset
Pirenópolis, Goiás, Brazil

📷 Canon EOS 5DS R, Canon 16-35mm lens, 1/10sec at f/16, ISO 250.
Tripod. Post-capture: basic image management.

The sun was setting over the vast tropical savanna of the cerrado, highlighting a field of *sempre-vivas* (Portuguese for 'everlasting' flowers), which are famed for their beauty in dried flower arrangements.

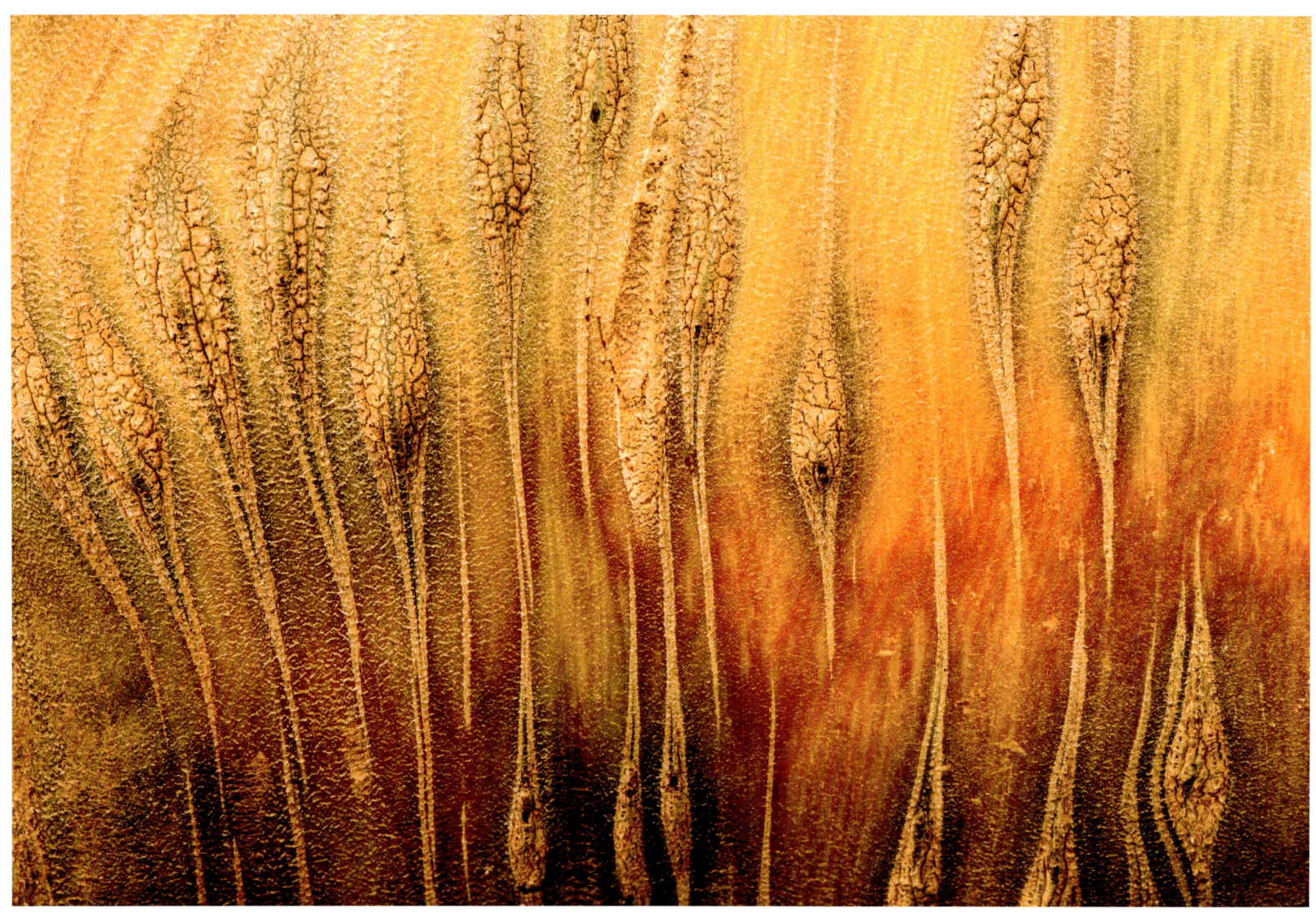

STEPHEN STUDD
1st Place

Giant Carrot
Malvern, England, UK

📷 Canon EOS 6D, Canon 180mm macro lens, 4sec at f/32, ISO 100. Tripod. Post-capture: basic image management.

Whilst at the giant vegetable competition at Malvern, I used a macro lens to capture the wonderful abstract patterns on display.

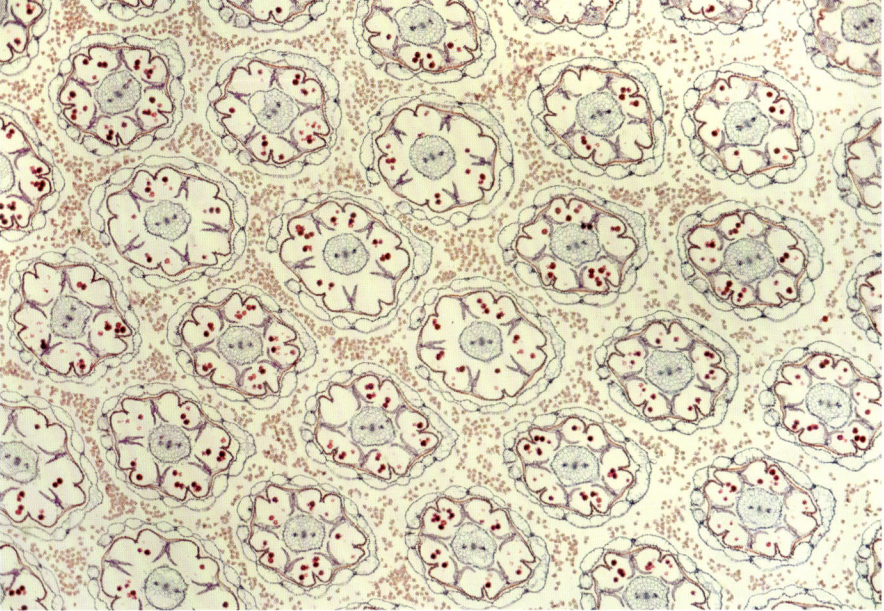

PETER PULLAN
2ND PLACE

The Creation
Bridgetown, Australia

📷 Canon EOS 6D, Canon 100mm macro lens, 1/100sec at f/11, ISO 400.
Post-capture: basic image management.

The bark of this *Eucalyptus* tree is redolent of Australian Aboriginal art in its simplicity, colour and abstraction.

STEVE LOWRY
3RD PLACE

Taraxacum officinale
Portstewart, Northern Ireland, UK

📷 Nikon D200, microscope objective lens, 1/640sec, ISO 100. Olympus BX45, cable release. Post-capture: basic image management.

This image shows a chemically stained cross-section of a common dandelion *capitulum*, displaying beautiful individual florets.

SIMON SCHOLLUM
1st Place

Pomegranate
Timaru, South Canterbury, New Zealand

Linhof M679, Phase One IQ260, Rodenstock 180mm lens, 1/30sec at f/22, ISO 100. Post-capture: basic image management in Capture One Pro 10.

I chose a cross-section of a pomegranate *(Punica granatum)* to feature as the central subject in this still life, which was captured at my home studio in New Zealand.

MANDY DISHER
2ND PLACE

Autumn Fruits
Cambridgeshire, England, UK

📷 Canon EOS 7D, Canon 50mm lens, 2sec to 8sec at f/23, ISO 100. Tripod.

The colours and textures of mini pumpkins and *Physalis alkekengi var. franchetii* pods lent themselves perfectly to an autumnal themed still life. The look and feel of the photograph was achieved using HDR, (High Dynamic Range) merging three individual exposures together.

BERT SHANKMAN
3RD PLACE

Sentient
Olney, Maryland, USA

📷 Olympus OM-D E-M5 Mark II, Panasonic Leica 45mm macro lens, 1/4sec at f/3.2, ISO 200. Post-capture: applied digital manipulation.

Although a still life aims to capture a moment of arranged beauty from subjects no longer growing, I wanted to illustrate a pervasive sense of life.

TIMOTHY SMITH
FINALIST

Japanese Gardens
National Trust Tatton Park,
Cheshire, England, UK

📷 Canon EOS 5D, Canon 24-105mm lens,
1/50sec at f/11, ISO 200. Infrared filter.
Post-capture: basic image management.

I had purposely chosen to visit the
Japanese Garden in Tatton Park
as I had read they were one of the
finest in the country. They did not
disappoint. Everything was in place
for a dramatic shot. The water lily
leaves broke up the foreground and
added some tonal interest but it
was the bridge and pagoda which
underpinned the entire composition.

LIU WUPIN
FINALIST

Leaf Frog on Vein
Dabie Mountains, China

📷 Nikon D3S, Tamron 90mm lens, 1/60sec at f/16,
ISO 800. Post-capture: basic image management.

It was summertime when I captured
this scene of an upturned lily leaf and
tree frog in the Dabie Mountains. I
was initially attracted to the beautiful
network of leaf veins but when I
kneeled down to get a closer look the
frog climbed on to the leaf to rest;
I was careful not to disturb it as I
composed the shot.

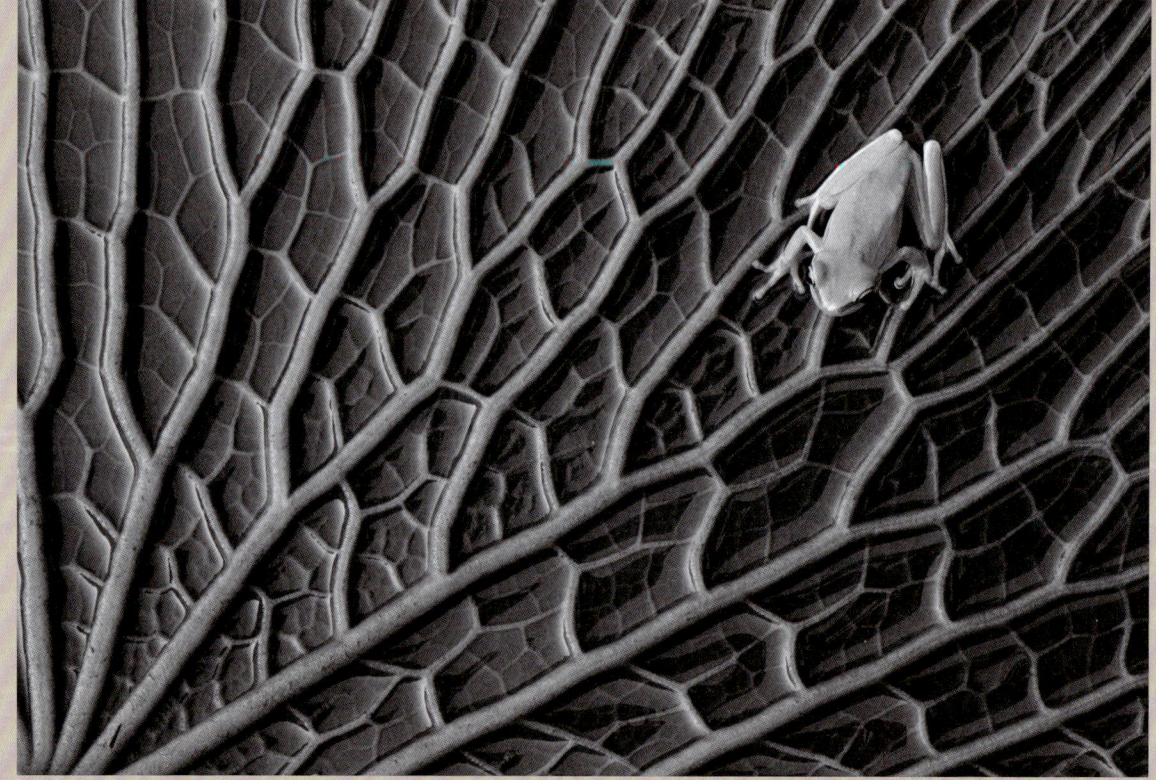

BRONWEN KEY
FINALIST

Mesmerise
Wellington Botanic Garden, New Zealand

📷 Canon EOS 6D, Lensbaby Velvet 56mm lens, 1/250sec at f/2, ISO 100.
Post-capture: basic image management.

I took this shot looking down into the centre of a cactus. Shooting in black and white really helped emphasise the contrast between the spines and wool, creating a mesmerising composition.

REGINA HELENA RASO BASTOS
FINALIST

Mirror
Rio de Janeiro Botanical Garden, Brazil

📷 Canon EOS 50D, Sigma 70-200mm lens, 1/2000sec at f/7.1, ISO 200.
Post-capture: basic image management.

I love reflections because they have the capacity to double the beauty and magic of a subject. The flower of the *Victoria amazonica* is a masterpiece of nature and I knew I had to capture it.

JANE DIBNAH
FINALIST

Aquilegia
Shropshire, England, UK

📷 Canon EOS 7D Mark II, Canon 180mm macro lens, 1/640sec at f/5, ISO 400. Tripod, reflector. Post-capture: basic image management.

The falling stamens and graceful lines of the petals created a wonderful sense of movement.

TRUI HEINHUIS
FINALIST

Dancing Poppies
Goor, The Netherlands

📷 Nikon D4, Nikkor 105mm macro lens, 1/4000sec at f/3.2, ISO 400. Post-capture: basic image management.

I captured this poppy in the early morning sun, its fragile form dancing in the wind.

BOB LUIJKS
FINALIST

Waiting
Ospel, The Netherlands

📷 Canon EOS 5D Mark III, Lensbaby Velvet 56mm lens, 1/5000sec at f/2, ISO 100.
Post-capture: basic image management.

I found this spider just after sunrise with its web glistening in the morning light. I used a cooler looking white balance to create a more dramatic scene.

ALISON LAWRENCE
FINALIST

Dandelion Droplet
Bourton-on-the-Water, England, UK

📷 Nikon D600, Nikon 105mm macro lens, 1/4sec at f/10, ISO 100. Tripod, remote release.
Post-capture: basic image management.

I love photographing dandelions and am always trying to capture something different. I sprayed this one with water and luckily enough an escaping seedhead caught a dazzling droplet.

ROBIN NOORDA
FINALIST

Ultra-Vanity
Amsterdam, The Netherlands

📷 Nikon D810, Nikkor 24mm tilt-shift lens, 30sec at f/11, ISO 400. Tripod, remote release, LED torch with UV filter. Post-capture: focus stacked three exposures, basic image management.

UVIVF (Ultraviolet-Induced Visible Fluorescence) allows certain structures to glow with magic and interest. This is particularly noticeable on the artichoke, cornflower, fossil ferns and the seeds of the sunflower.

FLAVIO CATALANO
FINALIST

Red Tomatoes
Turin, Italy

📷 Nikon D750, Nikkor 105mm macro lens, 0.5sec at f/2.8, ISO 100. Tripod. Post-capture: basic image management.

Tomatoes are the main summer vegetable crop here in Italy. They truly are products of the sun, so I used natural light to capture their character and beauty.

GRAHAM LOVE
FINALIST

Past Times
Stonegate, East Sussex, England, UK

Fujifilm X-T2, Fujinon 100-400mm lens, 1/25sec at f/4.8, ISO 6400. Tripod.
Post-capture: basic image management.

I picked *Lathyrus odoratus* (sweet pea) flowers from my garden to feature in this still life composition. I added a distressed background that was exposed with natural sunlight from my kitchen window.

POLINA PLOTNIKOVA
FINALIST

In Glory of Pumpkins and Gourds
London, England, UK

Canon EOS 5D Mark II, Canon 24-70mm lens, 1/125sec at f/5.6, ISO 100. Tripod, studio lights.
Post-capture: basic image management.

I arranged these pumpkins and gourds in the style of paintings by the old Dutch Masters for a compelling still life.

LOTTE GRØNKJÆR-FUNCH　　　　　　*Physalis alkekengi,* Black & White

SIMON HADLEIGH-SPARKS　　　　　　**New Day,** Black & White

ZSOLT VARANKA
Ice Flower, Macro Art

VERONICA BARRETT
Declining Gracefully, Macro Art

STEVE LOWRY
Nymphaea, Macro Art

JUDITH BORREMANS **Marbled White,** Macro Art

MINGHUI YUAN **Lace,** Macro Art

HAZEL ELLIS **Monarch,** Macro Art

ANDREA GARUFFO *Macroglossum stellatarum,* Macro Art

BERT SHANKMAN   **Monkeyshine,** Still Life

INNA KARPOVA   **Study of Lemons,** Still Life

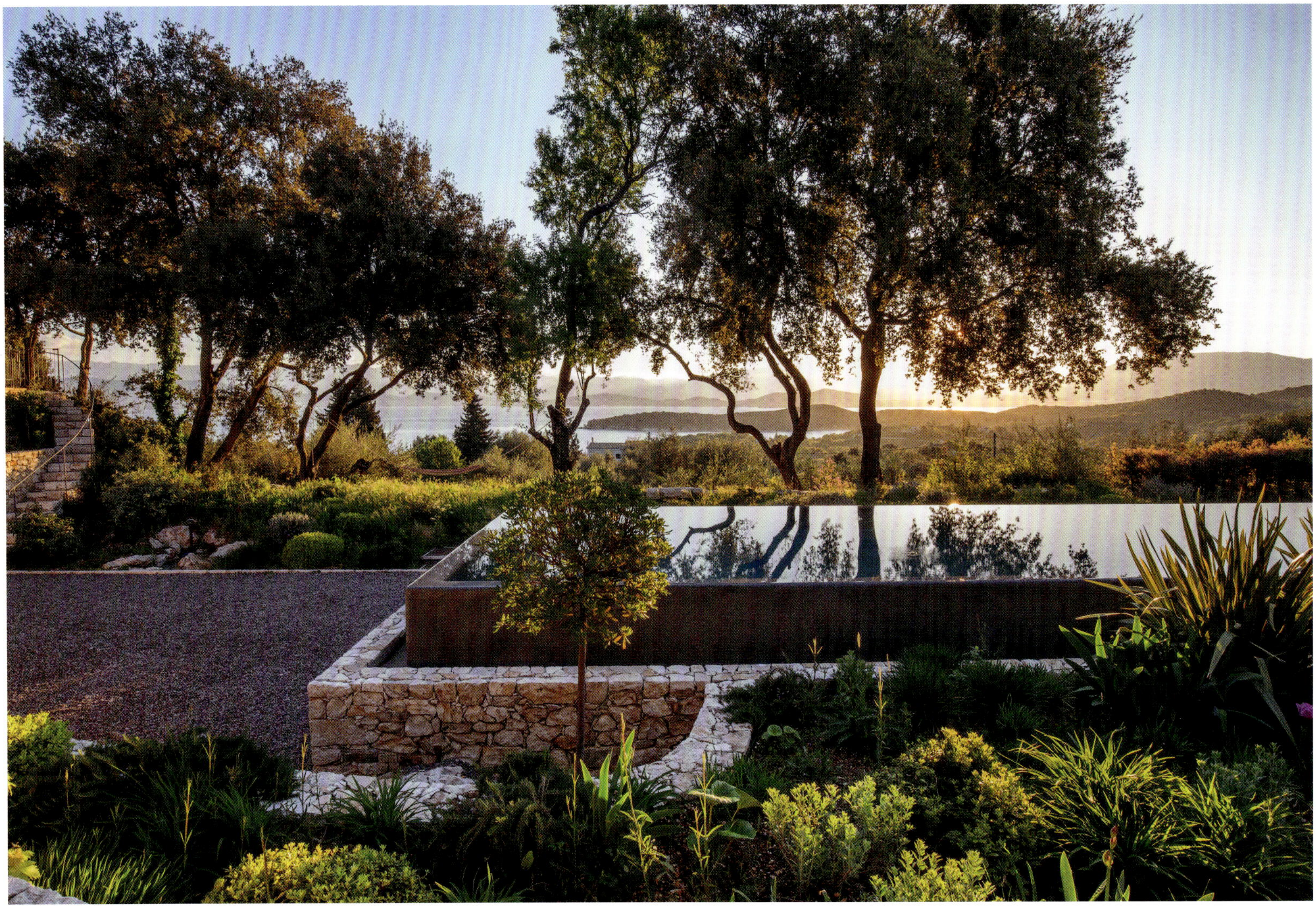

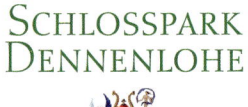

MARIANNE MAJERUS
1ST PLACE

Mediterranean Dawn
Corfu, Greece

📷 Canon EOS 5D Mark III, Canon 16-35mm lens, 1/30sec at f/16, ISO 400. Tripod.
Post-capture: basic image management.

The Mediterranean sun was rising over a contemporary terrace garden, flooding the frame with warm light. The background trees provided perfect sun shields whilst the pool reflected their shape and form in the still, inviting water.

SCHLOSSPARK
DENNENLOHE

European
Garden Photo
Award

DANIÈLE DUGRÉ
2ND PLACE

Autumnal Impressions at the Red Bridge
Schlosspark Dennenlohe, Bavaria, Germany

📷 Nikon D600, Nikkor 24-120mm lens, 0.3sec at f/22, ISO 125. Tripod. Post-capture: basic image management.

At Schlosspark Dennenlohe there are many wonderfully themed areas to explore, all with their own unique character, planting and colour schemes. The *Rhododendron* Park features a red bridge as a contrasting centrepiece to the lush summer shrubs and trees.

RACHELE ZSCHOCK-CECCHINI
3RD PLACE

Late Afternoon
Ort im Innkreis, Upper Austria, Austria

📷 Sony α77V, Zeiss 50mm lens, 1/50sec at f/14, ISO 200. Post-capture: basic image management.

Late afternoon sunlight highlighted the features of this nursery garden in Upper Austria, highlighting colour, textures and a sense of passing time.

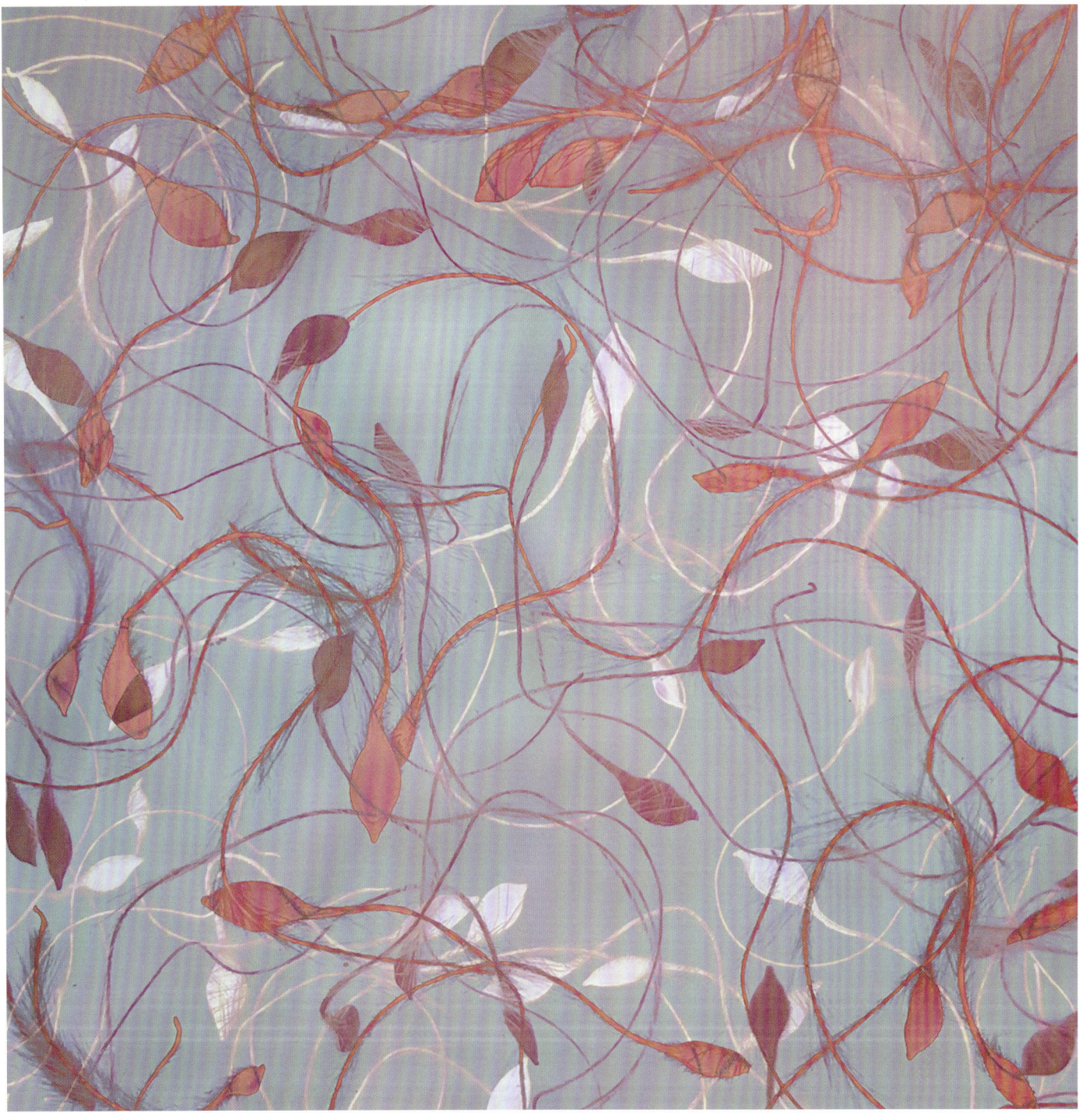

JANE SIMMONDS
1ST PLACE

Seed Doodles
Gloucestershire, England, UK

📷 Apple iPhone 7 Plus, 1/590sec to 1/480sec at f/1.8, ISO 20. Lightbox.
Post-capture: blended together multiple images, basic image management.

I blended together multiple images of *Clematis* seeds from my garden to create an artistic and intriguing composition.

KERSTIN SCHELBERG

2ND PLACE

Red-Flowering Currant

North Rhine-Westphalia, Germany

 Apple iPhone 6s, 4sec at f/2.2, ISO 200. Slow Shutter Cam app.
Post-capture: blended together multiple images in Snapseed app, basic image management.

I used the iPhone app, Snapseed, to blend together multiple images of the red-flowering currant plant *(Ribes sanguineum).*

ANNALAURA PRETAROLI

3RD PLACE

Kew Lights

Royal Botanic Gardens, Kew, London, England, UK

Apple iPhone SE, 1/35sec at f/2.2, ISO 50.
Post-capture: basic image management.

Kew is wonderful at any time of the year, but is especially magical at Christmas time when the Gardens are illuminated with festive lights.

ZYGMUNT SZOT

1st Place

The Sackler Crossing

Royal Botanic Gardens, Kew, London, England, UK

Pentax K-1, Pentax 15-30mm lens, 1/2500sec at f/6.3, ISO 800.
Post-capture: basic image management.

It was a very cold January morning in Kew Gardens as I stood on the north side of the lake, watching the sunrise over the Sackler Crossing. The vibrant reds of the foreground *Cornus* beautifully complemented the hues of the morning sky. The crossing was named after philanthropists Dr Mortimer and Dame Theresa Sackler, whose donation made its construction possible.

Royal Botanic Gardens
Kew

TAMMY MARLAR
2ND PLACE

Fully Loaded
Royal Botanic Gardens, Kew, London, England, UK

📷 Canon EOS 5D Mark III, Canon 180mm macro lens, 1/1600sec at f/5, ISO 400.
Post-capture: basic image management.

A near fully laden bee continued to collect pollen from these autumn *Crocus*, despite the heavy load.

PAULA COOPER
3RD PLACE

The Hive
Royal Botanic Gardens, Kew, London, England, UK

📷 Panasonic Lumix DMC-G80, Lumix 14-140mm lens, 1/13sec at f/5.6, ISO 200.
In-camera multiple exposures. Post-capture: basic image management.

I wanted to explore a different aspect of this much-photographed structure. I decided to use the in-camera multiple exposure function to show the link between the surrounding wildflowers and The Hive itself.

ALISON STAITE   **Autumn Poppy,** Captured at Kew

JOHN MATHER   **Hive Tree,** Captured at Kew

SUSAN HONEYWELL   **Storm Clouds,** Captured at Kew

ALISON STAITE   **Pasqueflower,** Captured at Kew